Introduction to the Mac
All Sorts of Handy Tips

MacOS 13 Ventura Edition

© 2023 iTandCoffee

Special Sales and Supply Queries

For any information about buying this title in bulk quantities, or for supply of this title for educational or fund-raising purposes, contact iTandCoffee on **1300 885 420** or email **enquiry@itandcoffee.com.au**.

iTandCoffee classes and private appointments

For queries about classes and private appointments with iTandCoffee, call **1300 885 420** or email **enquiry@itandcoffee.com.au.**

iTandCoffee operates in and around Camberwell, Victoria in Australia.

Introducing iTandCoffee ...

iTandCoffee is a Melbourne-based business that was founded in 2012, by IT professional Lynette Coulston.

Lynette and the staff at iTandCoffee have a passion for helping others - especially women of all ages - to enter and navigate the new, and often daunting, world of technology and to utilise technology to make life easier, not harder!

At iTandCoffee, **patience is our virtue.**

You'll find a welcoming smile, a relaxed cup of tea or coffee, and a genuine enthusiasm for helping you to gain the confidence to use and enjoy your technology.

With personalised appointments and small, friendly classes – either remotely, in our bright, comfortable, cafe-style space or at your own place - we offer a brand of technology support and education that is so hard to find.

At iTandCoffee, you won't find young 'techies' who speak in a foreign language and move at a pace that leaves you floundering and 'bamboozled'!

Our focus is on helping you to use your technology in a way that enhances your personal and/or professional life – to feel more informed, organised, connected and entertained!

Call on iTandCoffee for help with all sorts of technology – Apple, Windows, Android, iCloud, Evernote, OneDrive, Office 365, Dropbox, all sorts of other Apps, getting you set up on the internet, setting up a printer, and so much more.

Introducing iTandCoffee ...

If you are in small business, iTandCoffee has can help in so many ways – with amazing affordable solutions for your business information needs and marketing.

Here are just some of the topics covered in our regular classes:

- Microsoft Office Products and Microsoft 365 – OneDrive, Word, Excel, PowerPoint
- Introduction to the iPad and iPhone
- Bring your Busy Life under Control using your technology.
- Getting to know your Mac and The Photos app on the Mac
- Understanding and using iCloud
- An Organised Life with Evernote
- Taking and Managing photos on the iPhone and iPad
- Managing Photos on a Windows computer
- Windows basics
- Travel with your iPad, iPhone and other technology.
- Keeping kids safe on the iPad, iPhone and iPod Touch.
- Staying Safe Online
- Making the most of your personal technology in your business

The iTandCoffee website (itandcoffee.com.au) offers a wide variety of resources for those brave enough to venture online to learn more: handy hints for iPad, iPhone and Mac; videos and slideshows of iTandCoffee classes; guides on a range of topics; a blog covering all sorts of topical events.

We also produce a regular Handy Hint newsletter full of information that is of interest to our clients and subscribers.

Hopefully, that gives you a bit of a picture of iTandCoffee and what we are about. Please don't hesitate to contact iTandCoffee to discuss our services or to make a booking.

We hope you enjoy this guide and find its contents informative and useful. Please feel free to offer feedback at feedback@itandcoffee.com.au.

Regards,

Lynette Coulston (iTandCoffee Founder)

Introduction to the Mac
All Sorts of Handy Tips
TABLE OF CONTENTS

Introduction to the Mac
All Sorts of Handy Tips

TABLE OF CONTENTS (cont.)

Before we start

About this guide

In this fourth guide of the **Introduction to the Mac** series, we share all sorts of great tips that will help you to get so much more from your Mac – and help you troubleshoot when your Mac is a bit slow or misbehaving.

A great companion to this guide – providing more tips than we can ever cover in a guide like this – is our online **Mastering the Mac** set of tutorials, available on the iTandCoffee Website.

Visit www.itandcoffee.com.au/apple-mac-videos for more information.

Click, Double-click and Right-Click

Throughout this guide, we will often refer to the 'Click' and 'Right-click' gestures.

Refer to Part 1 of this series of **Introduction to the Mac** guides, called **A Guided Tour**, for more details of how to set up your **Mouse and Trackpad** in **System Settings** to support your preferences for these gestures.

When we refer to 'Click', we are talking about the standard single left-click on the Mouse or a single-finger click on the main area of the Trackpad. 'Double-click' means two 'clicks' in quick succession.

(Note. This assumes a 'right-handed' setup for your Mouse! You can set up your Mouse to switch sides for the 'click' and 'right-click' gestures if you are left-handed. See **A Guided Tour** for more on this.)

This 'click' and 'double-click' could instead be a 'tap' or 'double-tap' if you have enabled this feature in the **System Settings** for your **Mouse** or **Trackpad**.

Where there are references to the **'right-click'** gesture, this is referring the 'right-click on the Mouse' gesture – called the **secondary click** in **System Settings -> Mouse,** or **Trackpad**.

This the same gesture as the **Control-click** keyboard shortcut, the **two-finger click** gesture on the trackpad, and the **bottom right corner click** gesture on the trackpad (if you have chosen this instead of the 'two-finger click').

In some places in the document, we mention all of the 'secondary click' gestures when we refer to 'right-click'. But in cases were where we only mention the 'right-click', please substitute the gesture that applies on your own Mac.

Before we start

Scrolling

For those of you who are using a MacBook and its Trackpad, don't forget that scrolling up and down is achieved by dragging two fingers up and down on your trackpad, and one finger up and down on your Magic Mouse.

Refer to the guide **A Guided Tour** for more details about setting up your Mac's Trackpad gestures.

New in macOS Ventura

Throughout this document, we have updated any references to System Preferences (pre-Ventura) to instead refer to System Settings (new in Ventura) and to show the relevant screens from the new System Settings.

There are various settings that we reference in this document that have moved – for example, those relating to Keychain and Passwords, Login Items, Storage management. See the descriptions in this document for further information.

Taking Screen Images
(Screen Capture)

Keyboard Shortcuts to Capture your Screen

This is a feature that I use multiple times every day.

You can take a photo of whatever is on your screen – either the entire screen, or a selected part of the screen.

These screen images can be saved to your Desktop as a file or can just go into your computer's 'clipboard' (an area of memory), ready to be pasted into an email, document, or somewhere else.

Taking an image of the screen involves the consecutive pressing of several keys.

Comm-Shift-3	Take photo of the full screen and store in a file on the Desktop.
Comm-Shift-Ctrl-3	Take photo of the full screen and save it in the Clipboard.
Comm-Shift-4	Select an area of the screen to copy to a file on the Desktop.
Comm-Shift-Ctrl-4	Select an area of the screen to copy to the Clipboard.
Comm-Shift-4, **then Space Bar**	*(i.e. Combination of the 3 keys, then let go and press Space.)* Click on the window that is to be copied to a file on the Desktop
Comm-Shift-Ctrl-4, **then Space Bar**	*(i.e. Combination of the 4 keys, then let go and press Space.)* Click on the window that is to be copied to the Clipboard

When your image is in the Clipboard, just choose **Command-V** to paste it as an image into another place. Or create a new image by opening **Preview** and selecting **File -> New from Clipboard.**

Any screenshot file created will have a name format as shown in the image on the right – i.e. it will include the date and time that the image was taken.

Screen Shot 2020-12-04 at 12.06.16 pm.png
Screen Shot 2020-12-06 at 2.00.16 pm (2).png
Screen Shot 2020-12-06 at 2.00.16 pm.png
Screen Shot 2020-12-06 at 9.21.06 am.png
Screen Shot 2020-12-06 at 9.21.24 am.png
Screen Shot 2020-12-06 at 9.21.29 am.png

Taking Screen Images (Screen Capture)

'Floating Thumbnail' for screenshots

Since macOS Mojave, when you take a screenshot that creates a file, you will see some handy features in relation to that new file. (Note. This only applies if a file is created – not for screenshots that go to the clipboard.)

Just like on your iPhone, a small thumbnail of your screenshot will then appear - at the bottom right of the screen. This thumbnail will disappear after a few seconds if you do nothing with it.

Here's what you can do with that thumbnail while it is still on the screen.

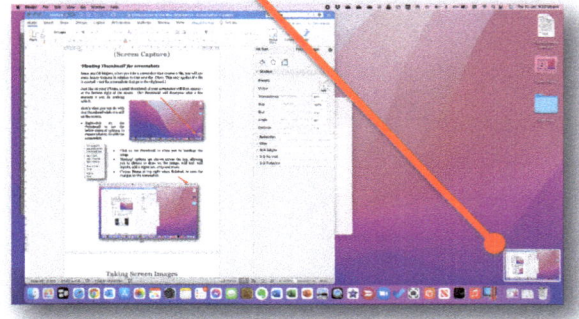

- Right-click on the thumbnail to see the below menu of options, to choose what to do with the screenshot.

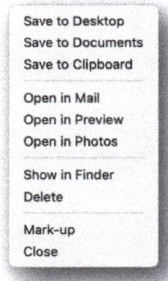

- Click on the thumbnail to allow you to 'markup' the image
- 'Markup' options are shown across the top, allowing you to choose to draw on the image, add text, add objects, add a signature, crop and more (covered soon).
- Choose **Done** at top right when finished, to save the changes to the screenshot.

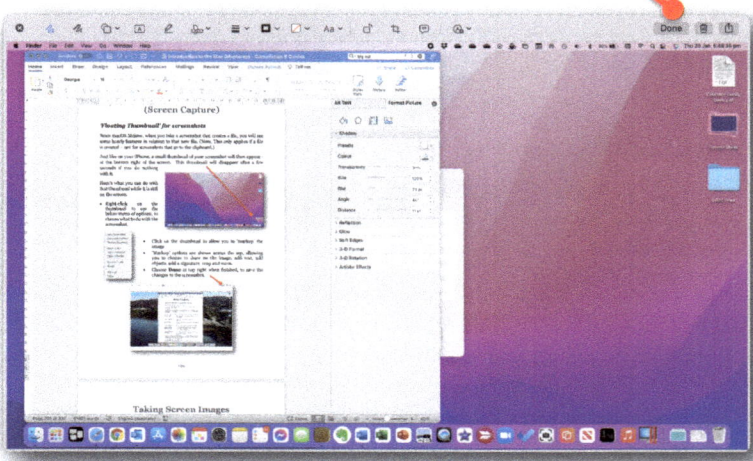

Taking Screen Images (Screen Capture)

The screenshot will save to your Desktop (or to an alternate location if you have chosen one – see how you do this in the next sub-section).

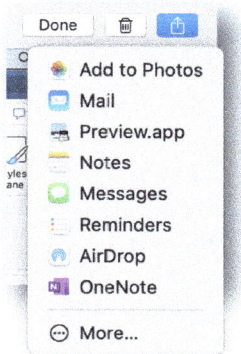

Alternatively, choose the **Share** symbol on the far top right of the Markup screen to see a set of places where you can choose to share or save the screenshot.

If you choose from one of the options shown here, the screenshot will not be automatically saved to the Desktop (as it normally would when you choose **Done**).

In the next section, we look at how to turn off this 'floating thumbnail' if you don't want it to appear.

Screen Capture Menu

macOS Mojave introduced some new functionality in relation to screen shots, which is activated using the keyboard combination **Command–Shift–5**.

Command-Shift-5 will provide a set of options towards the bottom of the screen, that allow for the selection of the type of screen capture that you require – including the option to record a video of all or part of your screen.

Hover the cursor over each option to see what the symbol means.

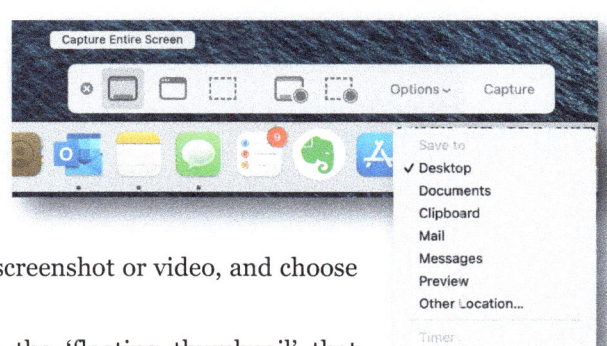

The **Options** menu allows you to set a timer (to delay the capture of the screenshot), to choose where to save the screenshot or video, and choose your microphone settings.

If you don't wish to see the 'floating thumbnail' that appears at bottom right whenever you take a screen shot (or screen video), untick the **Show Floating Thumbnail** option.

Click the **Capture** option once you have chosen the type of screen shot to take.

Insert a Photo from your iPhone/iPad

Another feature available since macOS Mojave is the ability to take a photo or scan a document on your iPad or iPhone and import it directly to your Mac – perhaps to the desktop, into another folder, directly into a Mail message, into a Note or elsewhere.

To take and import a photo to a folder or your desktop, right-click in a vacant space on your Desktop or in Finder and choose **Import from iPhone** (iPad) and **Take Photo**. Alternatively right-click on a folder in Finder to add the imported content to that folder.

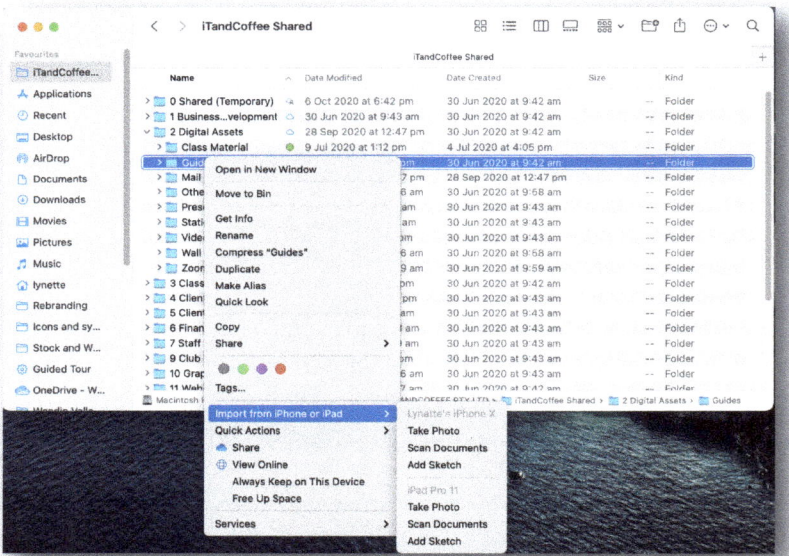

If it is a document that you wish to scan and automatically crop with your iPhone/iPad, choose the **Scan Documents** option.

Similarly, when drafting an email or Note, right-click in the body and choose the same options.

If only one i-Device is available, you may just see the **Take Photo** option (and no **Import from iPhone or iPad** option).

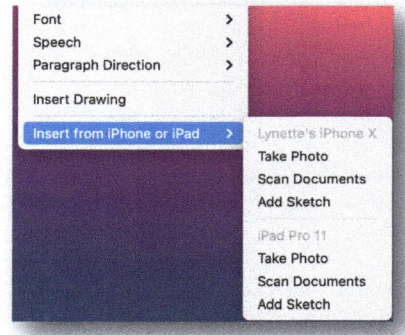

8

Quickly Tidying a Messy Desktop

If you, like me, take lots of screenshots, you quickly can end up with a desktop that is very messy, covered in icons of folders and files.

A messy, cluttered desktop can have a performance impact on your Mac.

Since macOS Catalina, there has been an easy way of cleaning up your untidy Desktop.

Simply right-click in a vacant space on the Desktop and click **Use Stacks**.

Your screen will magically arrange its content by type of file.

Once you click (to tick) the **Use Stacks** option, right clicking on a vacant space again will show that you now have the **Group Stacks By** option – to choose how you would like to use the **Stacks**.

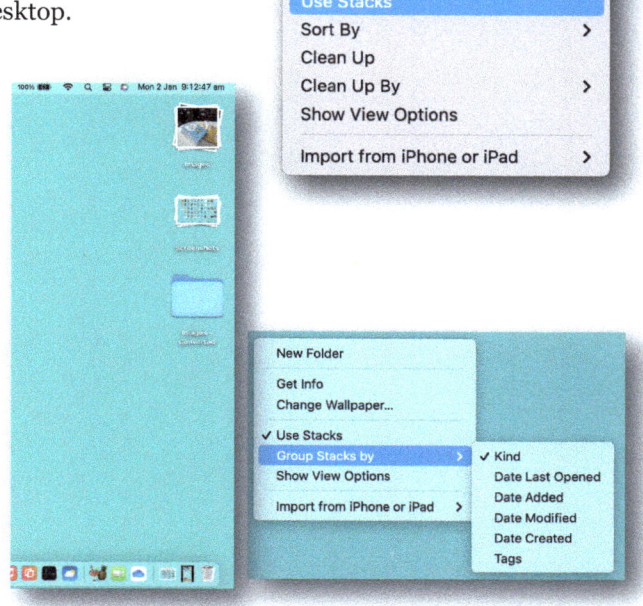

9

Quickly Tidying a Messy Desktop

To view the contents of any 'Stack', simply click on it.

A 'down-arrow' icon replaces the Stack, and all items are shown.

To collapse the Stack again, click on that down-arrow icon.

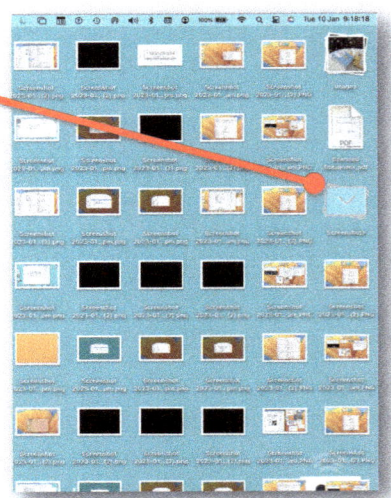

If the items in the are no longer needed, right-click on the Stack and move the whole Stack to the Bin by

- Clicking it and choosing **Command-Delete**,

- right-clicking and choosing **Move to Bin** or

- dragging the Stack to the Bin at bottom right.

Or, if you want to save the content of that stack, use the top option of the right-click menu to create a new folder that is made up of the content of that Stack.

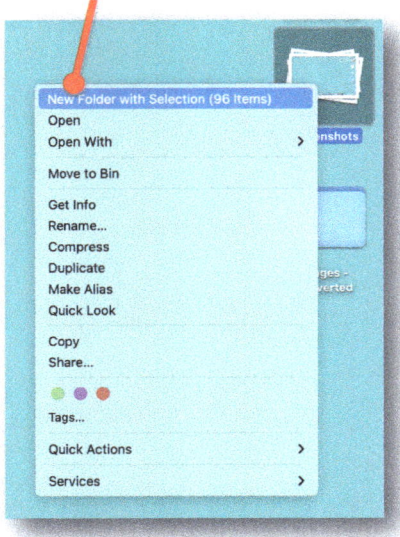

Creating a PDF from any image/s or document

PDF stands for 'Portable Document Format'. Files in this format can be read on any computer or mobile device. A PDF is a document in its 'print format'.

Certain apps on your Mac that allow you to create documents, spreadsheets images and presentations, will allow you choose to 'Save As a PDF' or 'Export as PDF'.

For example, you may use Microsoft Word on your Mac to create documents.

If you sent a Microsoft Word document to someone via email, that person may not be able to open the document if their device doesn't have Microsoft Word installed. Even if they can open the document in an alternative app, it may not appear with the formatting that you have so carefully applied.

The solution is to send this document as a PDF instead of the MS Word document, since PDF is a format that can be read by any device.

In MS Word, Excel and PowerPoint, if you want to create a PDF version of your document, choose the **File -> Save As** option, then choose the 'file format' of **PDF.**

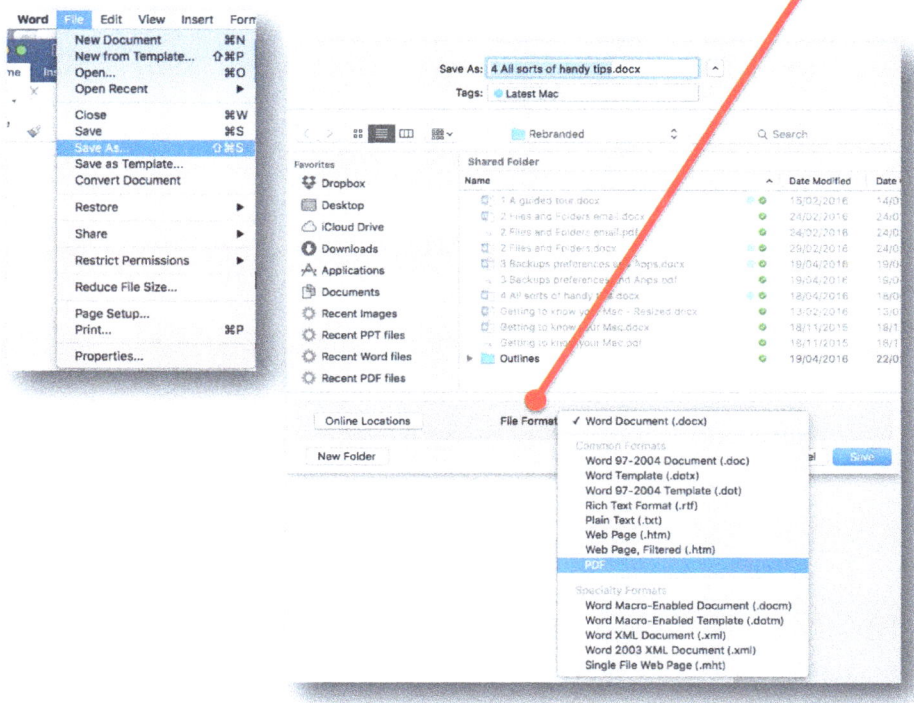

Creating a PDF from any image/s or document

In Apple apps like *Pages, Numbers* and *Keynote*, look for the **Export To** option in the **File** menu, and choose **PDF.**

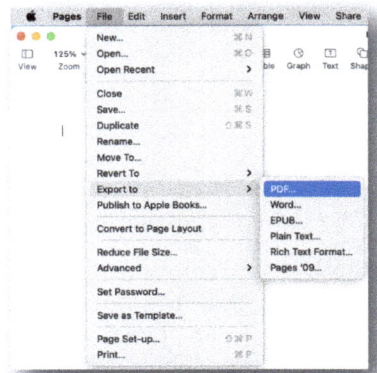

(You will see here that you can also export Pages documents to Word – useful if you need to send a Pages document to someone who needs to edit it using Word instead of Pages.)

When you create a PDF document, you are effectively 'printing' the document to a file, instead of to the printer – so the PDF file has all the formatting that you would see in the printed version.

If you ever want to choose to only 'print' part of a document to the PDF file, this is achieved from the **Print** option in the **File** menu.

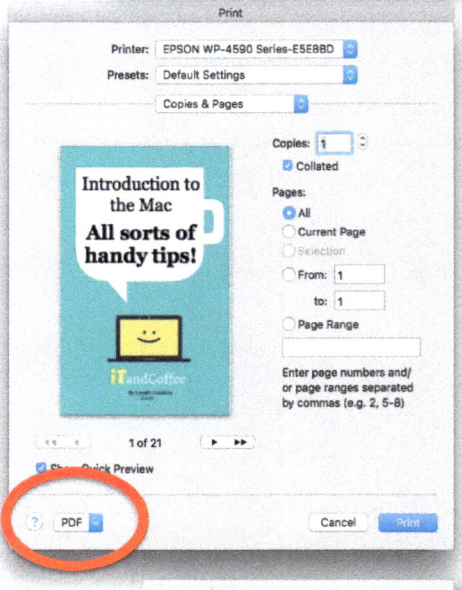

Choose the relevant options that you would choose to print the document – paper size, orientation, page range.

Then, choose the **PDF** option at the bottom left (circled in image on right).

This will offer several options for the PDF's creation:

- Open PDF in Preview,
- Save as PDF
- Mail PDF
- Send PDF via Messages
- And more.

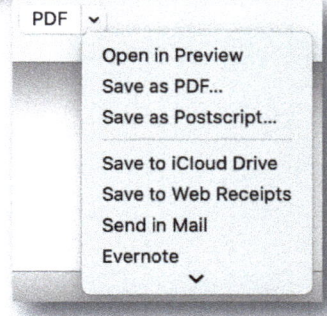

By using the Mail PDF option, you can send a PDF version of a file without having to first save it.

The Preview App
Viewing & Editing Images/PDFs

Preview is a wonderful built-in App on your Mac, one that allows for the viewing and editing of PDFs and Images.

This means that you don't need a third-party app (such as Adobe Reader) for this purpose.

Preview has a treasure trove of features:

- Change a file to a different format – for example, change a PDF file to a jpeg image.
- Create an image from a frame in a video.
- Remove a background
- Adjust colour and exposure
- Add annotations to a PDF or image.
- Sign documents and save your signature for future signings.
- Reduce the file size of a PDF or image.
- Merge multiple files into one PDF
- Rotate pages in a PDF
- Crop a PDF or image.
- Fill out and create PDF forms
- Password-protect a PDF or image
- Get an image of an App icon
- Sign and annotate a document that is part of a Mail message.

Let's look at some of these features of Preview...

The Preview App
Viewing & Editing Images/PDFs

Change a PDF or image file to alternate format

This is something that I need to do on a regular basis. Quite often, I have a file that is a PNG format, but need it to be in JPEG format. Or, I have a PDF that needs to be saved as an image.

To do this, choose **File->Export**, then choose the required format from the options at the bottom, in **Format**.

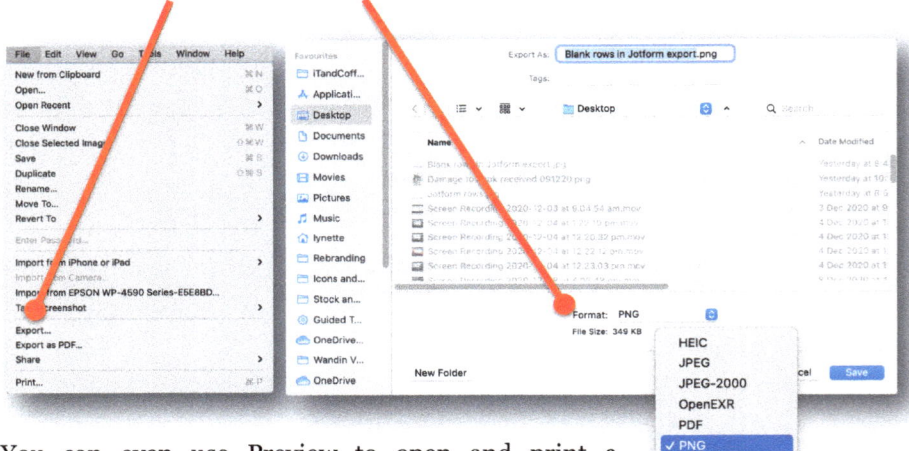

You can even use Preview to open and print a Photoshop or Illustrator file, and to export such a file to a different format.

If the original file is a 'vector-based' logo or illustration – which means that the image can be resized without losing its quality – the PDF that you generate using Preview will also be vector-based.

The Format options that are normally shown in the **Format** list are limited to the most commonly used.

To see the full set of available formats, simply hold the **Option** key when you click on the Format list box. Then, you will even be able to save a PDF or image to Photoshop or PostScript format.

The Preview App
Viewing & Editing Images/PDFs

Reduce a PDF file size

A PDF that has, say, been created from a Word or Pages document can often be very large – mainly due to the size of the images in the PDF.

To reduce the file size, choose **File->Export**, then choose the **PDF** format.

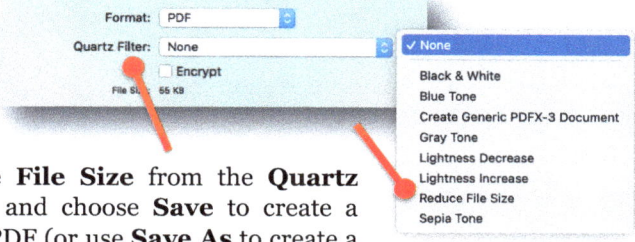

Then, choose **Reduce File Size** from the **Quartz Filter** set of options, and choose **Save** to create a smaller version of the PDF (or use **Save As** to create a copy so that you don't lose the original).

Change the size of an image

This is something that I need to do regularly, when adding images to the iTandCoffee website.

In cases where the size of the image is larger than desired (since website images should have as small a file size as possible), I open the image in Preview and choose **Tools -> Adjust Size**

I can then adjust the dimensions of the image, usually choosing to adjust height/width by a 'percent' or 'pixels'. Click on the option on the right (as indicated below) to choose a different adjustment measure. Click **OK** to apply the size adjustment, then **File -> Save** to save the changes.

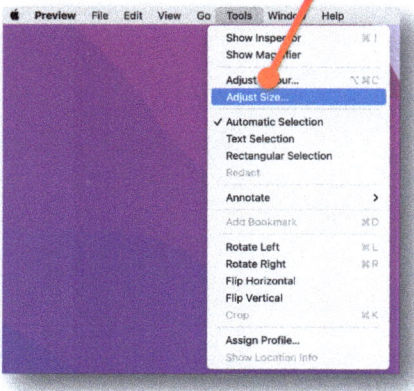

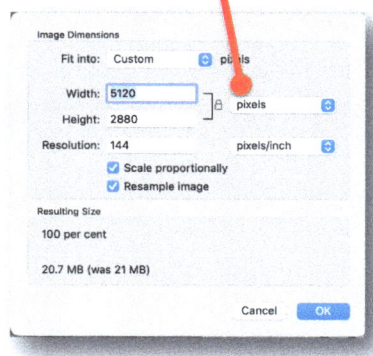

The Preview App
Viewing & Editing Images/PDFs

Merge multiple PDFs into one PDF

Preview makes it so easy to combine several PDFs into a single PDF, and to re-arrange the order the pages of that PDF.   Here's how to do it.

Open one of the PDFs that you wish to use.

Choose **View -> Thumbnails** to see small images of each page in the sidebar.

Drag the content of other files being viewed in Preview in the same way, or from the Desktop or Finder, into the position required.

You can use single or multiple page PDFs of any dimensions, or even add in images.

Then, rearrange the 'thumbnails' in the sidebar to reorder the pages – drag each page up or down to its required position in the list of thumbnails.

Once you are done, choose Save to save new combined PDF as a single file.

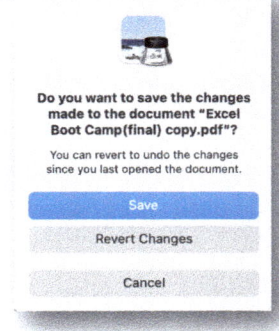

Or, if you wish to keep the original version, choose Export to export to a separate file.

If you don't want to save changes you have made to the file, on exit – when you get the message shown on right – choose **Revert Changes** instead of **Save**.

The Preview App
Viewing & Editing Images/PDFs

Merge multiple images into a single PDF file

If you have several images that you would like to merge into a single PDF, use the same method as described above for merging PDFs.

Instead of just 'saving', you will need to 'Print' the set of files as a single PDF. Choose **File->Print**, and then choose the **PDF** option at the bottom of the print screen (as described earlier).

Choose the **Save as PDF** or **Open PDF in Preview** option.

Rotating pages & images

If the 'orientation' of a page in your PDF needs adjusting (or your image is the wrong way up or around), Preview allows you rotate the page or image.

To rotate a single page, choose **View > Thumbnails** and then select the thumbnails of the pages you want to rotate.

Click the **Rotate** option in the toolbar or choose **Tools > Rotate Left** or **Tools > Rotate Right**.

Create a PDF or image from the Clipboard

If you have an image or some text copied to your Mac's Clipboard, the contents of the Clipboard can be used to create a file in Preview.

Just choose **File -> New from Clipboard.**

But where might you use this feature? Here's an example.

This option is great for cases where you took a video of an occasion but did not get a 'still' photo. Using a 'freeze frame' in the video, you want to create a photo.

The standard app for playing videos on your Mac is **QuickTime Player** (which we will look at further a bit later).

While playing the video in QuickTime, pause at the frame that you would like as an image, then choose **Command-C** (copy). This will place the image of the frame in the Mac's Clipboard.

The Preview App
Viewing & Editing Images/PDFs

Then, open **Preview** and choose **File->New from Clipboard**.

Then choose **File->Save** to save your image to the desired location on your Mac.

The standard format will be PNG, but this can be changed at the time of saving – to PDF, JPG, or another format.

Draw and write on a PDF

The 'Markup' option in the Preview toolbar will open up a toolbar that allows the addition of text and drawings to a PDF.

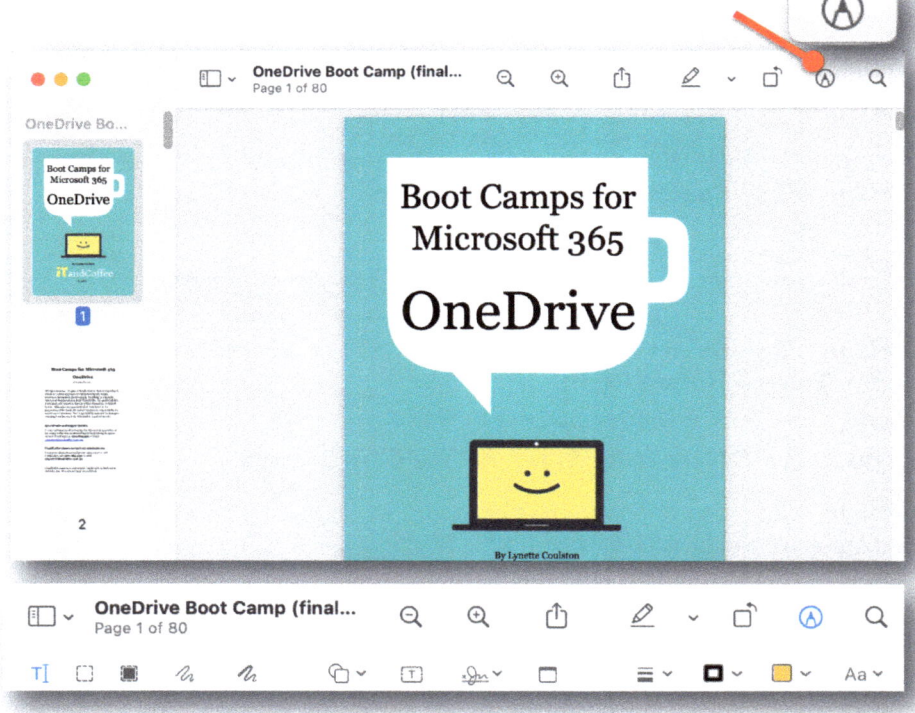

We won't go into all the options for 'annotating' your PDF, but here are some of the key things that you can do:

- Add a shape – filled or not filled, and with a line thickness that can be customized
- Draw arrows and lines
- Draw 'freehand'

The Preview App
Viewing & Editing Images/PDFs

- Highlight text in the document
- Add text to the document
- Add a signature to the document
- Crop a document

Crop a PDF page or image

Individual pages in your PDF, or your image that has been opened in Preview, can be Cropped.

This allows for the easy removal of page/image content that is not required.

Go into 'Markup' mode and click on the rectangular selection tool at top left.

Then click and drag to select the area that you wish to retain.

You will see a dotted border (see example below).

Choose **Tools -> Crop** OR choose the **Crop** option that appears in the toolbar when you select such an area.

The area outside the selected box will be deleted.

Choose **File->Save** to commit the changes.

The Preview App
Viewing & Editing Images/PDFs

Other forms of cropping

Of course, for images, you may not always want to perform a rectangular crop. You will notice a 'down-arrow' next to the rectangular selection tool when you are looking at an image in Preview.

This feature allows you to crop your image so that a 'circular' image remains (**Elliptical Selection**).

You can also draw line around the area that you want to keep, and remove the rest using **Lasso Selection**.

And **Smart Lasso** helps with this, by identifying the object/s that you probably want to keep when you draw a line around them.

Have a play with these options to see their effects.

Cropping the selected area instead of the surrounds

In some cases, you are actually wanting to crop the selected area instead of the area surrounding the selected area.

If this is the effect you are looking for then, instead of choosing the **Crop** option after selecting the area (as represented below left), press the **Delete** key. The image below right shows the result of selecting an elliptical area and then pressing the **Delete** key.

The Preview App
Viewing & Editing Images/PDFs

Remove a background

Sometimes, cropping is not enough!

Have you ever wished you could easily remove a background from an image, but thought that you needed an expensive tool like Photoshop to undertake such photo magic?

Preview can do this for you, using the **Instant Alpha** tool. It is the **'magic wand'** in the Markup toolbar. So click the Markup symbol to make sure it is blue, then click the wand so it too is blue.

As you click and drag, the Instant Alpha tool will select areas with the same colour. In the below example, I drag my cursor slightly in the speech bubble that has the question-mark.

The selected area will show as shaded (2nd image). When you let go, there will be a dotted outline around the area that is selected for removal (3rd image).

When I choose the Crop symbol, I get the fourth image - all other detail removed.

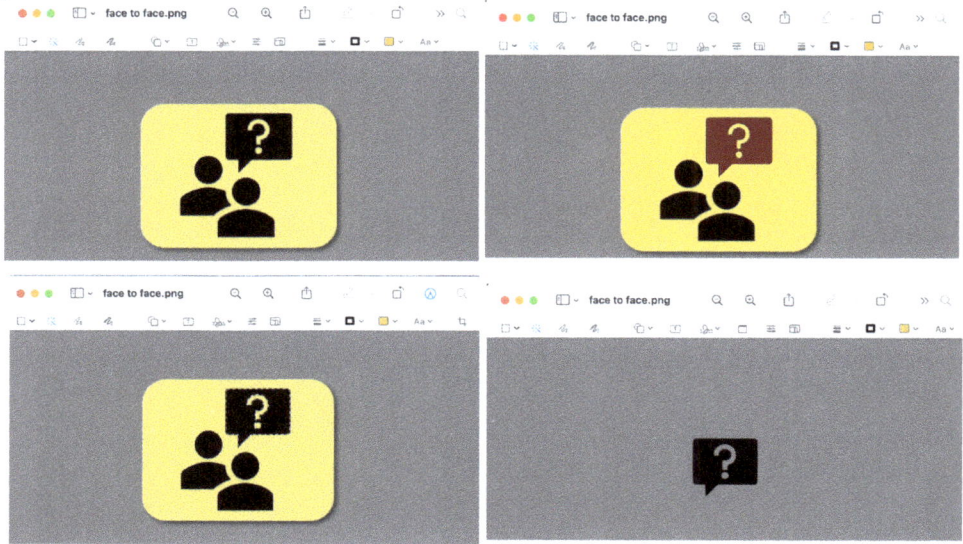

The Preview App
Viewing & Editing Images/PDFs

Or if I wanted to remove the yellow background, I would drag across an area where there is yellow. The selected area is then shaded orange.

When I let go, the dotted lines show the selected area (third image). If I choose the 'crop' symbol, all the black areas will disappear (as shown in the fourth image).

If, instead, I had chosen to press the **delete** key on the keyboard, the image on right would have resulted.

I could then select the yellow area of the question-mark and choose **delete** to get rid of that yellow.

When you are finished removing the unwanted background, save your image as a '.png' file – the format that allows for 'transparent' backgrounds.

The Preview App
Viewing & Editing Images/PDFs

Signing documents

The **Markup** toolbar has another handy feature that allows you to add your signature to a document.

Just choose the **Signature**  symbol from the Markup toolbar.

If you already have created a signature, click on the one that you wish to add to the document.

Otherwise, choose **Create Signature.**

Write your signature on a blank piece of paper.

Choose the **Camera** option at the top, then hold the paper with signature up in front of your Mac's Facetime camera.

When the signature is recognized on the line shown, select **Done.**

If you are not happy with it, choose **Clear** at bottom left and try again

If you have an iPad with an Apple Pencil or stylus, it is worth choosing the **iPhone or iPad** option.

Your iPad will then show a blank screen, ready for you to sign. As you draw on the iPad screen, you will see the signature appear on the Mac too.

Choose **Done** on the iPad or Mac when you have done this.

Click on the signature to add it to your document, then drag it to the required position and re-size as required.

This is especially handy when you do not have access to a printer and need to return a signed form – especially when you travel.

The Preview App
Viewing & Editing Images/PDFs

Quickly view any PDF or image with Quick Look

You can preview a PDF or image in Finder by clicking on it in the Finder list of files, and then pressing the **Spacebar.**

This will show the **Quick Look** window, which will display the contents of the file.

If the PDF has more than one page, you can scroll up and down to move through the pages.

At the top-right of **Quick Look** window is the option to **Open in Preview** and a **Share** icon, so you can send the PDF (or image) via Mail or Messages to another person.

Your Mac provides capability to 'markup'/annotate an image or document from this Quick Look screen – with a selection of the features that we just looked at for Preview.

Make Preview the default app for PDFs and Images

If you find that Adobe Reader has 'taken over' as the default application for PDFs (i.e. it opens whenever you double-click a PDF), you can change the default back to Preview if desired.

- Locate the PDF file in Finder and click it once to select it (but don't open it).

- Choose **File > Get Info** (or right-click to see this option).

- Click on the **Open With** drop down menu and choose **Preview** from the list of apps on your Mac that can open PDFs.

- Click **Change all** and confirm that you wish to change the default app.

The Preview App
Viewing & Editing Images/PDFs

PDF Permissions

A new feature added to Preview in macOS Monterey in 2021 was the ability to set permissions on a PDF.

These new settings are available when you **Save As**, **Export** or **Export As PDF** from Preview.

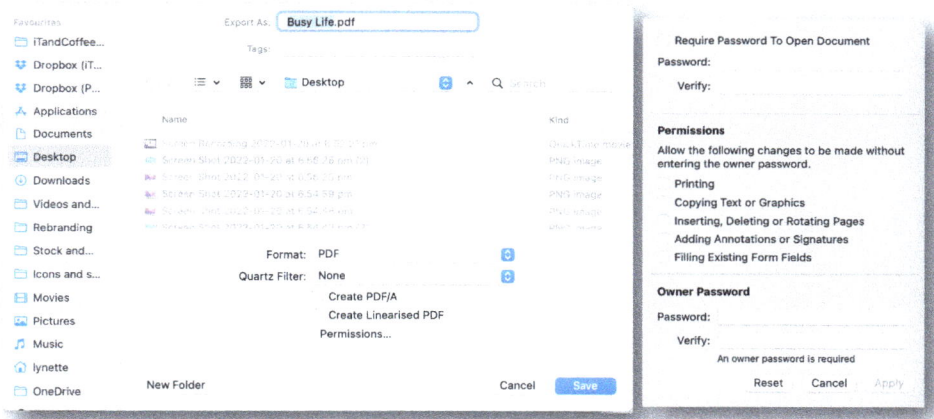

As shown in the image above right, you can optionally set the password for opening of the PDF, then decide what Permissions should apply to your Document from the list provided.

You must also set an 'Owner' password for the document (at the bottom).

Hidden Keys on the Keyboard

If you have ever wondered where to find certain keys and symbols, there are many, many keys 'hidden' on the Mac keyboard – but easily accessible using a combination of keys, as shown below.

French Accents

acute accent	é	Hold option key and e then **e**
grave accent	à, è, ù	Hold option key and ` then **a,e,u**
cedilla	ç	Hold option key and **c**
circumflex	â, ê, î, ô, û	Hold option key and i then **a,e,i,o,u**
tréma	ë, ï, ü	Hold option key and u then **e,i,u**
oe ligature	œ	Hold option key and **q**
French quotation	«	Hold option key and \
marks	»	Hold option key and shift key and \

Currency Symbols

Euro	€	Hold option key and shift key and **2**
British Pound	£	Hold option key and **3**
Cent Symbol	¢	Hold option key and **4**

Math symbols

Not Equals	≠	Hold option key and =
Infinity	∞	Hold option key and **5**
Approximately	≈	Hold option key and **x**
Pi	π	Hold option key and **p**
Less than or equal	≤	Hold option key and <
Greater than or equal	≤	Hold option key and >

Other Symbols

Degree symbol	º	Hold option key and shift key and **8**
Trademark	™	Hold option key and **2**
Registered	®	Hold option key and **r**
Copyright	©	Hold option key and **g**
Bullet point	•	Hold option key and **8**
Apple Symbol		Hold option key and shift key and **k**

Symbols and Emojis

Have you wondered where to find the 'Emoji' keyboard on your Mac - or perhaps you have had the need to include a symbol in a document, but not known where to find it?

The **Emoji and Symbol** window contains all sorts of Emoji's, symbols and pictures that can be added as a 'character' to any document or communication.

The window allows for the selection of any of the symbols shown by simply double-clicking on the applicable symbol. The symbol will then be inserted at the current cursor position.

Quick access to this Window can be achieved by adding it to the **Menu Bar.**

This can be done in **System Settings, from the Keyboard option.**

Select **Edit** on the right of the **Input Sources** option at top.

Select **All Input Sources** in the left sidebar, then turn on the **Show Input menu in menu bar** option.

Then, the symbol will appear in the status bar at the top of the screen.

Click this symbol and choose **Show Emoji and Symbols** (see first image on next page).

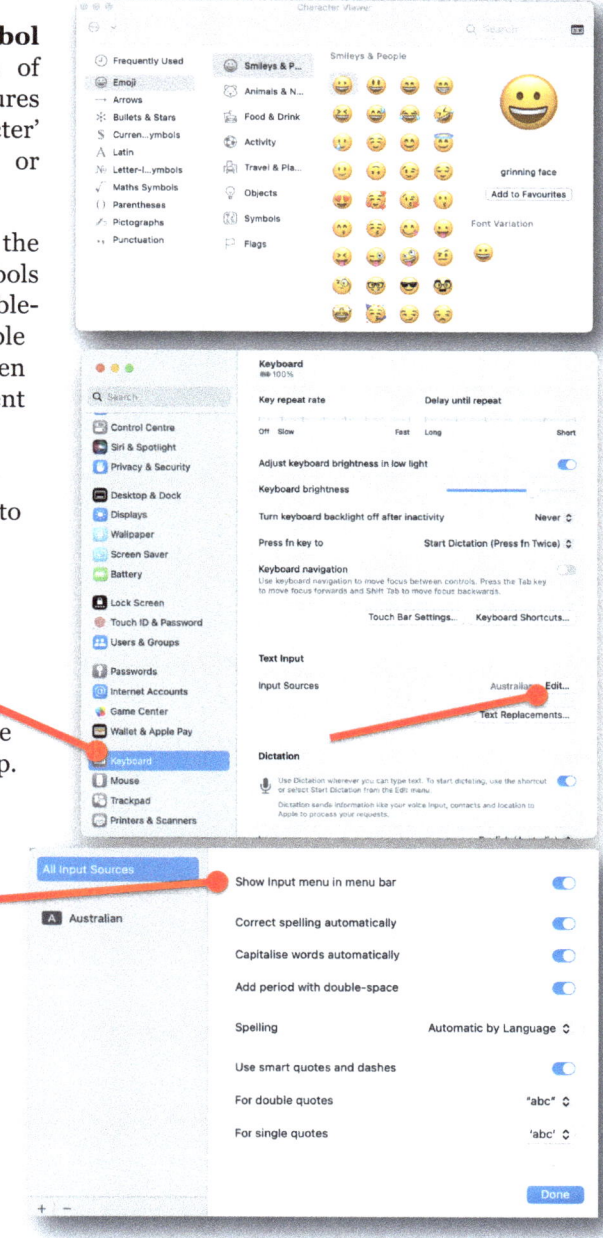

Symbols and Emoji

Alternatively, in the app that you wish to use a symbol or Emoji, go to the **Edit** menu in the top menu bar and look for the **Emoji & Symbols** option.

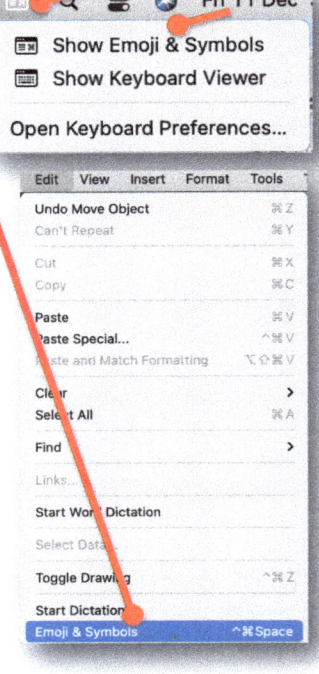

Or choose the Keyboard Shortcut **Command-Control-Space.**

All these methods bring up the **Character Viewer** window (see below)

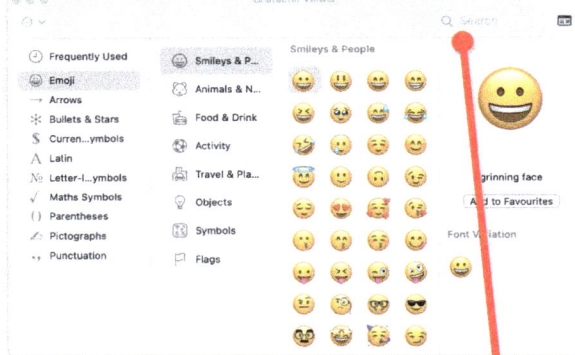

Use the Search bar at the top right of that window to find the perfect symbol.

To add one of these symbols to your document, email or text, simply set your cursor position and double-click on the symbol to insert.

Symbols can be resized and have their colour changed – just like any other character

You may find that when you choose this option, the screen you see is different to that shown above.

If the screen you see looks like that on the right, click the little icon at top right to see the full version of the screen.

.

28

QuickTime Player

Your Mac includes yet another hidden marvel of an App - one that you may have thought had just one simple function.

QuickTime Player is the app that will play your videos. It usually starts up whenever you double-click on a video file (assuming the video is in a format that Apple supports).

But QuickTime Player can do so much more than this. It can

1. Record a video using the Facetime camera of your Mac – choose **File -> New Movie Recording**
2. Record what is happening on your iPad or iPhone screen (audio and screen) – plug your iPad or iPhone into your Mac and choose **File -> New Movie Recording**
3. Make an audio recording – choose **File -> New Audio Recording**
4. Record what is happening on the Mac's screen, with or without Audio – for the whole screen, or just part of the screen. Choose **File -> New Screen Recording** (or use the new Screen Capture feature mentioned earlier, activated with the keyboard shortcut Command-Shift-5).
5. Change the format of a video or audio file (using the **Export As** option.

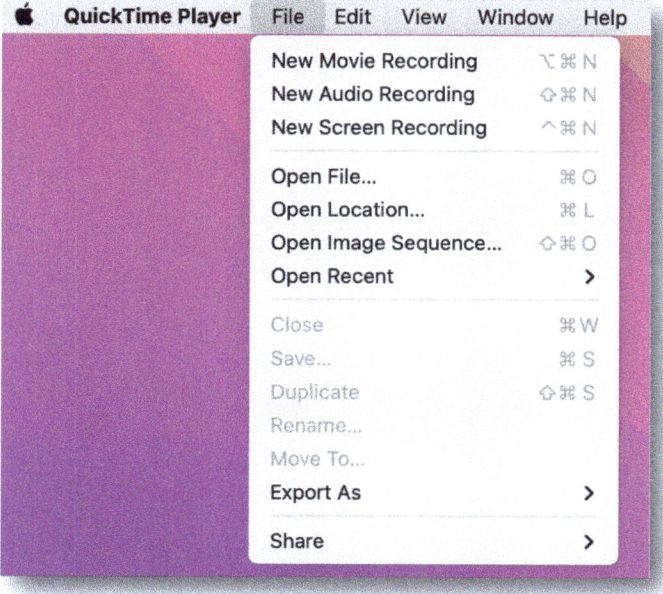

QuickTime Player

For an existing video, there are some other great functions, available in the **Edit** menu:

- Trim a video (start and end)
- Remove the video or audio
- Rotate a video
- Split a clip
- Add a clip to the end
- and more!

We won't go into further details of how to use this wonderful app here.

Perhaps have a play and discover for yourself the magic of QuickTime.

If you need further instruction on using this wonderful app, contact iTandCoffee.

Edit	View	Window	Help

Undo	⌘ Z
Redo	⇧⌘ Z
Cut	⌘ X
Copy	⌘ C
Paste	⌘ V
Delete	
Select All	⌘ A
Rotate Left	⇧⌘ L
Rotate Right	⇧⌘ R
Flip Horizontal	⇧⌘ H
Flip Vertical	⇧⌘ V
Clip Alignment	›
Split Clip	⌘ Y
Add Clip to End...	
Remove Audio	
Remove Video	
Trim...	⌘ T
Start Dictation...	
Emoji & Symbols	^⌘Space

Other Useful Built-in Apps

Maps

The Maps app closely resembles the same App on the iPad and iPhone.

Use it to find directions to somewhere, then send the 'route' details to your iPad or iPhone.

The Maps app is available from the **Launchpad** (if it is not already visible in your Dock).

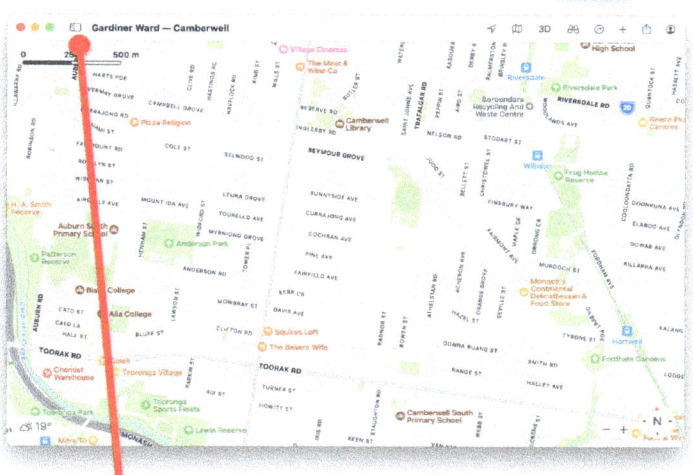

The view above is not showing the Maps sidebar – which can be exposed by clicking the symbol on the right of the traffic lights.

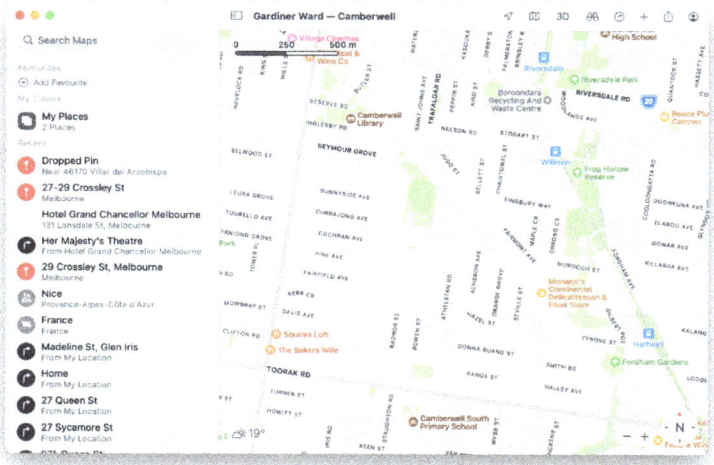

Other Useful Built-in Apps

The sidebar offers a Search field at the top. Just type in the name of a place, business or address to see the suggestions and to see it on the map.

On the top right, the right-angled arrow ⊙ allows directions to be requested for a from and to location.

Under that, the car, and other symbols allow for the choice of what sort of directions are required – driving, walking, public transport or bike tracks.

The folded paper symbol 🗺 allows the choice of view – whether you want the default Maps view, whether public transport routes are highlighted; whether you want to see the map in Satellite view.

In Satellite view, select the circled ... at bottom right and tick **Show Traffic** if you want to see current traffic 'snarls' as red or orange lines. (Note. This is option is no longer available for Driving maps – not sure why!)

To see your current location on map, click the ⊲ symbol.

Choose the 3D option to view your map in 3D.

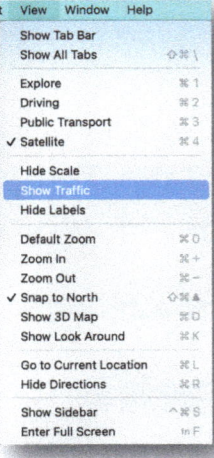

The View option in the (in the menu bar) provides another way of accessing the various ways of viewing your maps.

There is, of course, much more to this app! But we'll leave you to explore other features on your own.

Other Useful Built-in Apps

Digital Colour Meter

Have you ever wanted to reproduce a colour that is on your screen, and perhaps use it in some document or drawing that you are producing on your Mac?

Digital Colour Meter is a handy utility that can show the RGB (red, green, blue) coding of anything on the screen - great if you are trying to match a font or background colour.

It is found in your Launchpad, in the **Other** group of apps/utilities.

As for any other App or utility on your Mac, you can also open it easily by going to your Spotlight Search at top right 🔍 and starting to type the utility's name in the Spotlight Search bar.

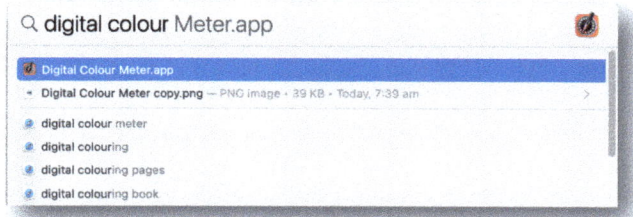

With the app active, just hover your cursor over the colour for which you need the RGB codes, and you will see the values appear in the **Digital Colour Meter** window.

In the below example, my cursor/arrow is pointed at the iTandCoffee logo – and the RGB code for that colour is shown by the Digital Colour Meter.

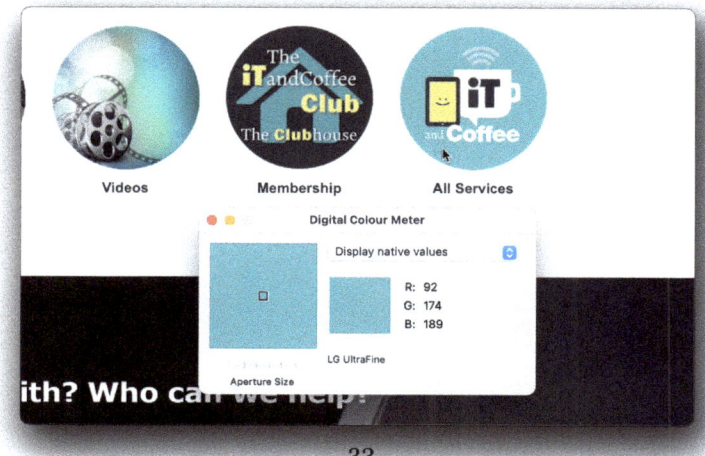

Other Useful Built-in Apps

Stickies

Stickies is a handy little standard App that allows you to 'stick' sticky notes to your screen! It is another utility that can be found in the Other group of Launchpad.

If you love your PostIt® notes, you will love the **Stickies** app.

To create a new Stickie, simply select **File->New Note** (or Command-N), then click on **Color** in the menu bar to choose the colour of your Note.

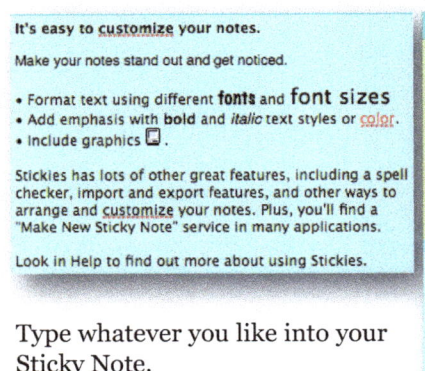

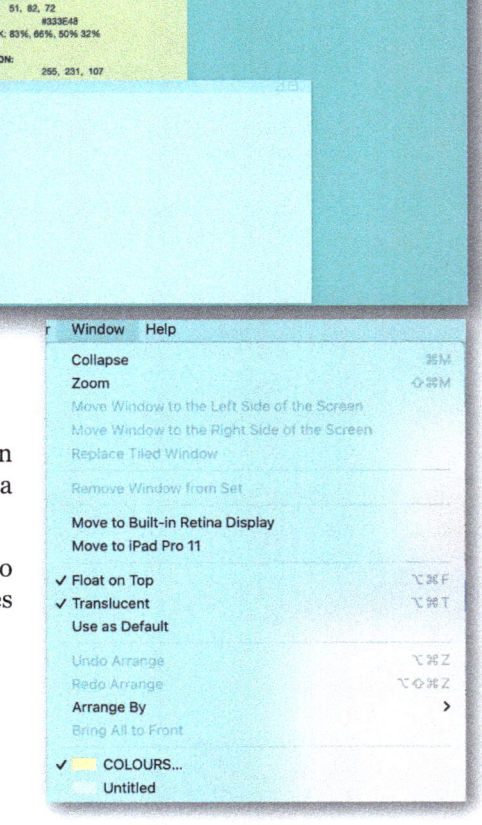

Type whatever you like into your Sticky Note.

Your Sticky Notes can be made to 'float' above all other windows (so they don't disappear and get forgotten).

From the **Window** menu, click on **Floating Window** (so that it shows a 'tick' on the left).

You will see there that you can also choose to make your Stickies **Translucent**!

Other Useful Built-in Apps

Keychain Access

Did you know that your Mac has a built-in 'Password Safe'?

What is a Password Safe?

It is a place to store all your important passwords (especially 'online account' passwords) so that they are available for viewing and use by various apps on your computer.

Your Mac's standard Password Safe is a utility called **Keychain Access.**

Whenever you visit a website and log in to an online account associated with that website (using an email address and password), you will be asked if you wish to save the login credentials to your Keychain.

Answering 'Yes' to the question will result in the details of the online account (web page, email address and password) being saved to your Keychain.

It is then possible to look up these saved account and password details by accessing the Keychain Access utility.

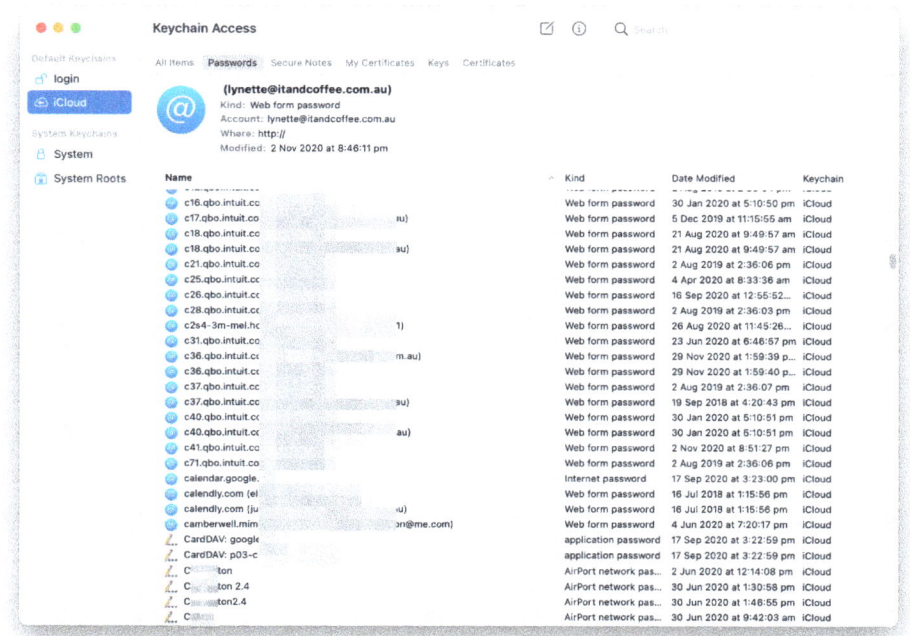

Other Useful Built-in Apps

Use the Search field at top right of the Keychain Access screen (see previous page) to type the 'domain' of the applicable website – or perhaps the email address that you used – and you will see a list of entries that match what you typed.

Find the account that you are looking for – double-click to open the item.

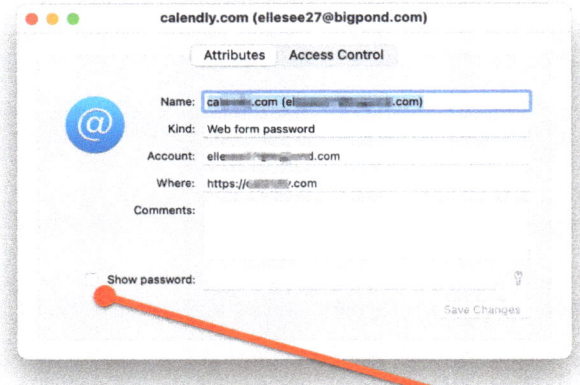

To view the item's password, click on the checkbox on the left of **Show password.**

You will be asked then to enter the user account password, in order to unlock this Keychain entry and reveal the password.

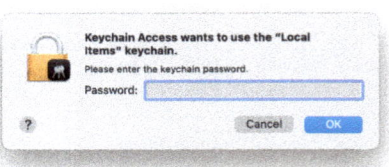

Your Keychain can be synchronized to your iCloud, so that it is then available on any other device that is also signed-in to that same iCloud account.

Visit **System Settings -> your-name** (Apple ID) **-> iCloud -> Password & Keychain** to set this up.

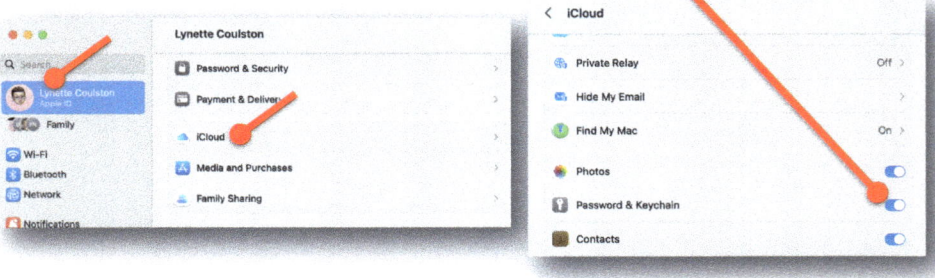

Other Useful Built-in Apps

View Passwords in System Settings

Since macOS Monterey, there has been an even easier way to look up and manage your saved Passwords.

System Settings includes the **Passwords** option.

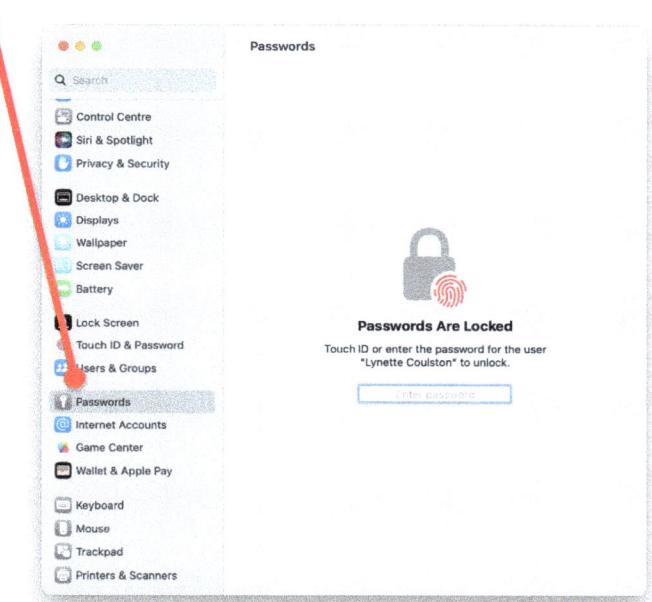

Select this option, then enter your Mac's password (or use your fingerprint to authenticate, if this has been set up). You will then see the list of passwords that have been saved.

Click on the ⓘ symbol on right of any entry to view details of that account and its password.

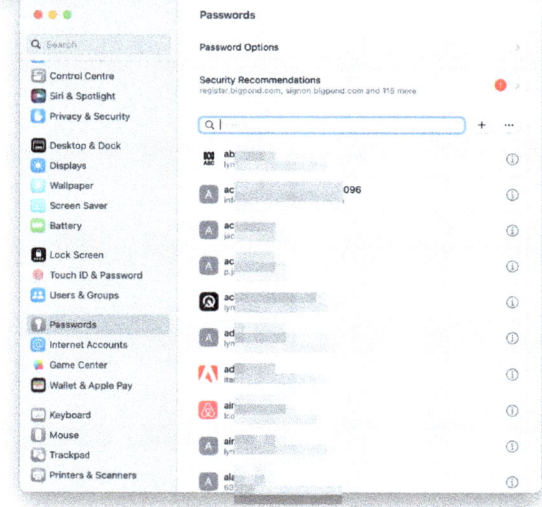

Other Useful Built-in Apps

Hover the mouse pointer over the dots that hide the Password to reveal this password.

Click on the revealed password to choose to Copy Password.

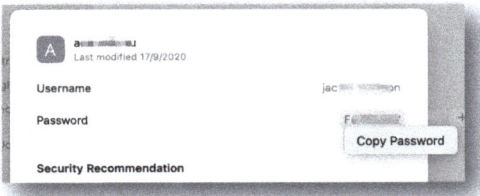

This offers a much quicker way of looking up those forgotten password and is much more user friendly than Keychain Access (which is still available if you need it)!

You can even manually add passwords for a particular website to this list, using the + symbol that is at the bottom of the list of passwords.

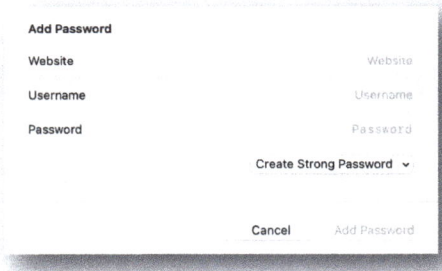

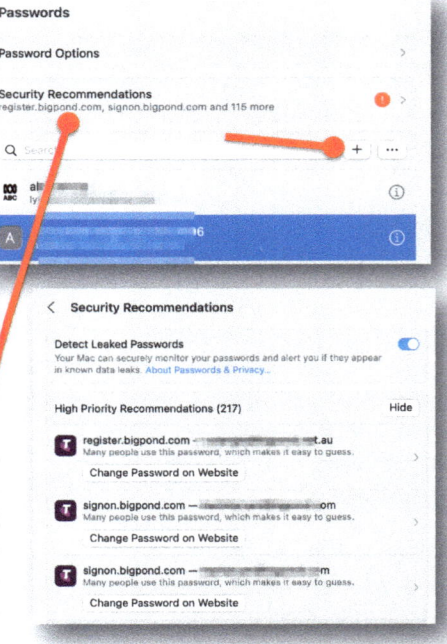

Not only can this new Passwords option help you find your passwords – it can also advise you of any passwords that might be compromised in a data leak, or that are too simple. It even provides a link to jump straight to the website to change a re-used, compromised or simple password.

You can disable the **Detect leaked passwords** feature using the option at the top (see image on previous page) – although I would leave this on, as it is a really useful feature.

Some Apps Worth Adding

DropBox, OneDrive, Google Drive

Much like iCloud, DropBox, OneDrive and Google Drive are Apps that can run on virtually any computer or mobile device – Windows, Mac, iPad, iPhone, Android, etc.

Their purpose is to allow the synchronization of files between computer/s and any other device that is signed in the same Dropbox, OneDrive or Google account.

Simply by storing files in the Dropbox, OneDrive or Google Drive folder on the computer, the files will also be 'synchronised' to the corresponding 'cloud' and then made available on any other device that is connected to the same account.

To set up **Dropbox** on your Mac, it is necessary to download its Mac app from **https://www.dropbox.com/downloading**.

OneDrive's Mac app can be obtained from the **Mac App Store**.

Google Backup & Sync can be downloaded from **https://dl.google.com/drive-file-stream/GoogleDrive.dmg**

Once installation of the relevant app is complete (and an account is created or signed in for the particular service), there will be a Dropbox, OneDrive or Google Drive folder visible s in Finder. At the time of writing this document, Dropbox still appears under Favourites in the left sidebar. The other services appear in the Locations section, further down in the left sidebar.

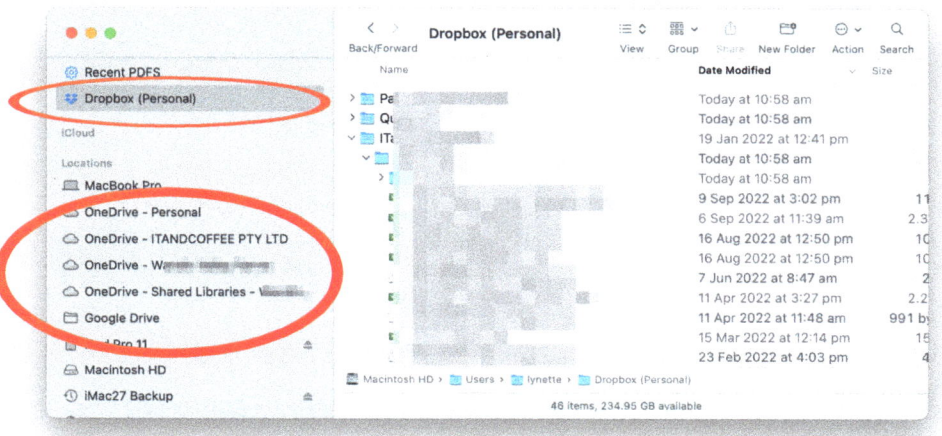

Just create your folder structure in that 'Cloud' library in Finder and store your files there.

Some Apps Worth Adding

Then you will have 'on the go' access to all your important information.

Another advantage of such Cloud Storage solutions is that they provide the ability to easily Share content with others – individual files or folders.

Additionally, they are available on all types of device – not just Apple devices.

Folders can be shared in such way that others can contribute to these folders and can edit the contents of the folder (if this is desirable).

Sharing is achieved by right-clicking on a folder or file and then choosing to Share a link, or from other Share options.

iTandCoffee has other guides on the topic of iCloud and OneDrive – see www.itandcoffee.com.au/guides for more information.

Handbrake

Handbrake is a popular app that allows for the 'ripping' of DVDs into a .mp4 file format, the conversion of videos from one format to another, and the compressing of large video/audio files.

I use it regularly to compress video handy hints and tutorials that I create. The .mov files created by Quicktime are generally very large, and Handbrake reduces them to a significantly smaller size.

Handbrake can be downloaded from **handbrake.fr**

Evernote, OneNote

Evernote and **OneNote** are wonderful apps that allow you to collect and catalogue information about all sorts of things. For example, recipes, articles, receipts, sporting fixtures, trip plans and itineraries.

While they are like the 'cloud' services mentioned earlier in their ability to share data between your Mac and your mobile devices, Evernote and OneNote are a lot more 'visual' – they are what we call 'digital scrapbooking app'.

Both **Evernote** and **OneNote** can be downloaded from the **Mac App Store**.

(Note. Even though I am still a big fan of Evernote for storing all sorts of information, Apple's Notes app has more recently become a real contender for the role of 'digital scrapbooking app – especially for those who are not going to need the more advanced features of an app like Evernote or OneNote.)

Some Apps Worth Adding

Skitch

Skitch is another app that can be downloaded from the **Mac App Store.**

Skitch is part of the Evernote Suite of apps and is a great app for annotating images and PDFs. Add arrows, pixelate private information, add shapes and text. It can then sync with your Evernote account – or export the updated image/PDF to a location on your Mac.

Owly

Owly is a free app that allows you to temporarily turn off your screensaver. I find this one very handy when I am running a class – where I don't want my screen to suddenly go blank in the middle of the class.

Owly can be downloaded from the **Mac App Store**.

Malwarebytes for Mac

Another form of protection that every Mac should have is a product that can check for, and remove, Adware and Malware.

Malwarebytes for Mac is a free app (although they do now prompt you regularly to upgrade to the paid version) that can rid your Mac of any such adware and malware Download it from **malwarebytes.org/antimalware/mac.**

VLC Player

If you have a video that won't play on your Mac, it is worth downloading the VLC Player app. Visit **videolan.org/vlc** to download.

Reflector

Reflector allows you to turn your Mac into an Apple TV, so that you can mirror your iPhone and iPad screens onto your Mac.

I find this very handy when presenting – being able to run a PowerPoint presentation on my Mac and being able to demonstrate iPad/iPhone functionality that is mirrored to the same Mac.

Some Apps Worth Adding

Canva

Canva is a wonderful online service with a corresponding Mac app, providing all sorts of image creation and editing capabilities, free stock photos, the ability to create invitations, thank-you cards, presentations, social media posts, and more. It offers lots for free, but a subscription is required for some of the more advanced features and content. It is definitely work checking out if you haven't already.

Zoom

Online meetings became such a feature of recent times, and one of the easiest apps that has become popular since the arrival of COVID is Zoom Meetings. Zoom is free to download and works on most computers, regardless of what version of the operating system is running.

Fixing a Slow Mac

Why is my Mac so slow?

They do say patience is a virtue but there is nothing more frustrating than a slow start-up of your MacBook or iMac, especially when it shouldn't take more than 30 seconds - normally!

And we are all familiar with the frustration of apps that take forever to start, or to do whatever it is they should do. That 'spinning beachball of death' can really raise the blood pressure.

While you may be tempted to download some third-party app (such as CleanMyMac or MacKeeper), these products can cause more problems than they solve, and really should be avoided.

If your Mac is quite old, it could be that nothing much helps to improve its performance – that it just can't cope any longer with the demands of newer versions of the Mac operating system. If the Mac only had 4GB of

Here is a list of things to try. In many cases that I deal with, the problem is resolved by one or several of these fixes.

How many apps and web pages are running right now?

Check your Dock to see how many apps have dots under them. The more apps you have running, the slower your Mac will operate. Quit any apps you are not using.

Also consider how many web pages you have open in **Safari** (or whatever web browser you use) and close any you are not using.

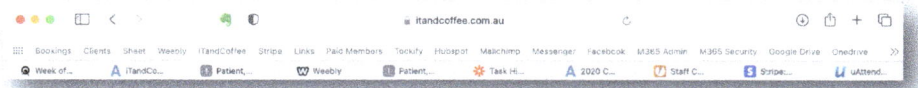

When did you last do a Restart

Sometimes, all your Mac needs is a re-start – especially if you haven't shut down or re-started in a while. This will clear out temporary files and caches and allow your Mac to start afresh.

Go to the menu (top left) and choose **Restart**.

Fixing a Slow Mac

Could it just be a very slow internet connection causing your issues?

Quite often I see clients who complain about a very slow Mac when, in fact, it is that that they have a very slow internet connection – and this is the cause of many of their issues with 'slowness'.

To check out the speed of your internet connection, visit **speedtest.net** and run a speed test. If you speed is below about 5mbps, it could be this which is causing your Mac's frustrating slowness in certain areas.

Are there multiple 'Users' logged in?

If your Mac has multiple User accounts, check if there is more than one User logged in at the moment. If there is, log out all other users.

Having more than one user logged in can really slow down the Mac, especially if the other user/s have apps running.

Auto-opening Apps on Login

Certain apps can be set up to automatically open whenever you log in to your Mac user account. This can mean that you have unnecessary apps running all the time.

This is the **Open at Login** option.

Some apps might turn on this **Open at Login** option when they are installed.

You can control which apps are allowed to **Open at Login** from your Dock (if that App appears in the dock).

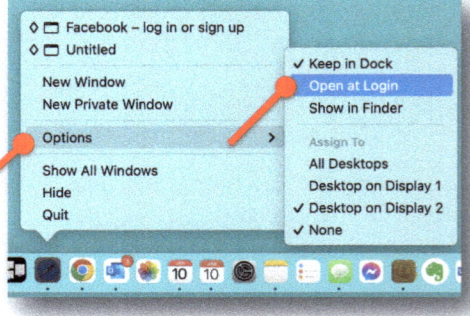

For Apps in the dock, right-click on app in the Dock and Choose **Options, Open at Login.**

If this option is 'ticked', then the App will open every time you log in. Click to untick if you don't want this to happen.

The list of apps that open every time you log in can also be managed from **System Settings->General->Login Items**.

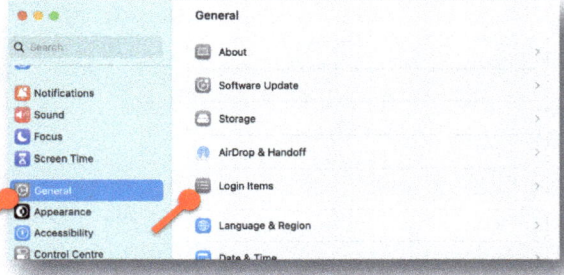

Fixing a Slow Mac

Click on any entry that you don't need to open on login and choose the minus – at bottom of the list.

Choose '+' to add a new App to the list, then select the App that you would like opened every time you log in.

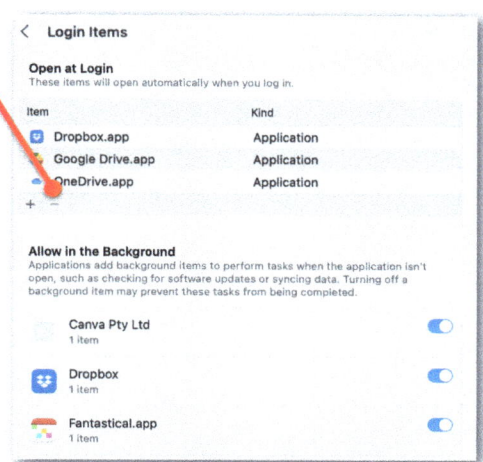

Quit apps when shutting down & re-starting

Apps and windows could be automatically opening as a result of what was open when you last shut down your Mac.

If you had 10 apps and files open, this would make your start-up time terribly slow too!

You can tell you Mac that you don't want this to occur, but you must do it at the time that you **Shut Down**, **Restart** or **Log Out.**

When you select -> **Shut Down,** -> **Restart**, or -> **Log out** *user-name,* a confirmation screen will appear.

You will notice that there is an option that is probably ticked - the **Reopen Windows when logging back in** option.

Simply 'Untick' this box to permanently turn off this feature for Restart, Login and Shut Down.

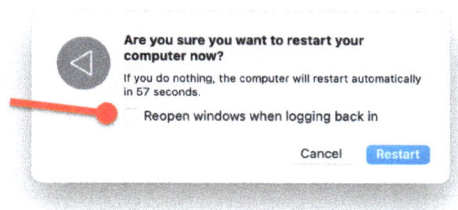

Fixing a Slow Mac

Is your Mac running low on disk space (new option in macOS Ventura)?

If your Mac is running out of storage space, its performance can be drastically impacted. It is easy to check how much disk space has been used.

A new option is now available in **System Settings**, under the **General** set of options – called **Storage**.

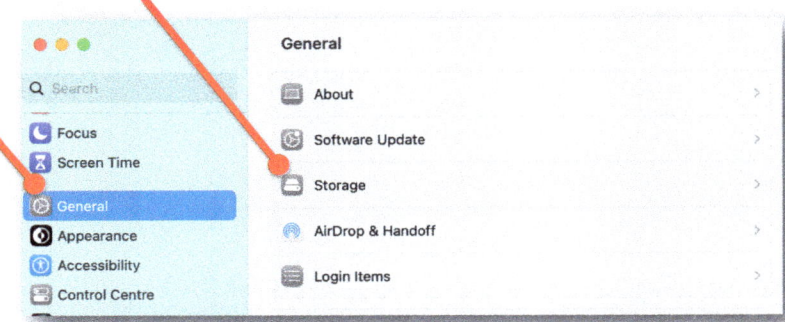

You will see a line representing your storage. Below that will be the list of areas where your storage is being used.

If you don't have much grey space on the right of the bar, you need to do some cleaning up of the contents of your computer.

As a rule, I always try to leave **AT LEAST 10GB free.**

Click on any items in the list below the bar to view the details of that area, sorted in order of biggest file first.

This allows you to see the size of individual items and, if any is not required, to **Delete** it or go to Finder to see the file in the context of its location.

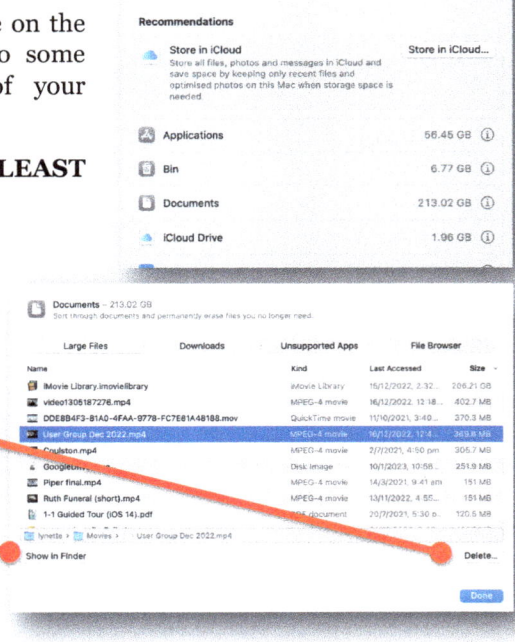

Fixing a Slow Mac

Check your Hard Drive's health with Disk Utility

Make sure there are no problems with your Mac's hard drive.

This can be done using **Disk Utility**.

Disk Utility is your 'go-to' app for some key functions relating to your Mac's hard disk drive (HDD), and for any other external storage devices that you attach to your Mac.

For example, if you can't eject a CD or USB, use **Disk Utility** to force eject it. Just click on the disk in the sidebar, then choose **File->Eject**

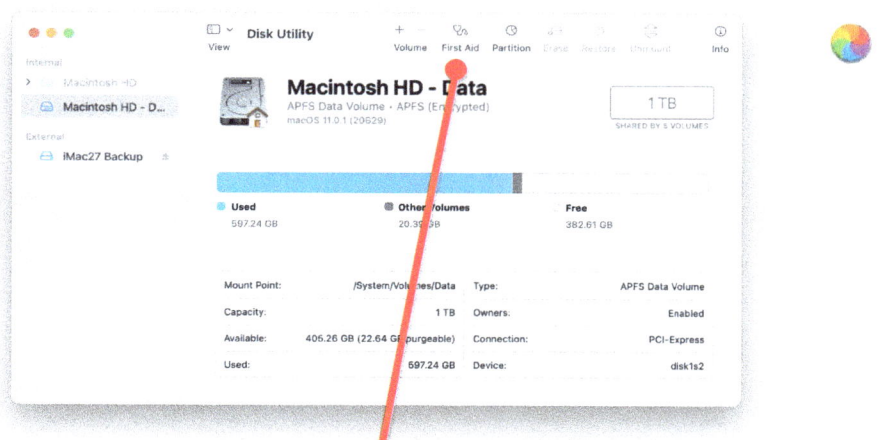

If your Mac is showing the '**spinning beachball of death**' on a regular and extended basis, it may be that you need to check the 'health' of your Mac's hard drive.

This is achieved by select the Macintosh HD in the left sidebar, clicking on the **First Aid** option along the top and then choosing **Run** to confirm that you wish to check it.

First Aid

If any problems are detected, Disk Utility will attempt to fix them, or notify of what to do next if a fix is not possible.

Larger problems may require that you run the utility in **Recovery Mode**, which can be accessed by restarting the computer and holding down **Command-R** until you hear the 'startup' chime and see the Apple symbol.

Fixing a Slow Mac

Follow the prompts until you see the **Recovery** menu, which shows the **Disk Utility** option.

After a successful repair, choose -> **Restart** to return to normal mode.

If a more serious problem in detected, it may be time for a visit to the Apple Geniuses!

Disk Utility also allows for the 'reformatting' of any external drive, through the **Erase** option. Be careful with this one – it will wipe all data from the device that you Erase.

Erase

Too much on the Desktop

Your Mac has to load up the icon of every single file on your desktop as it starts up.

It has to fetch all those icons and if you, like me, tend to accumulate a mess of a

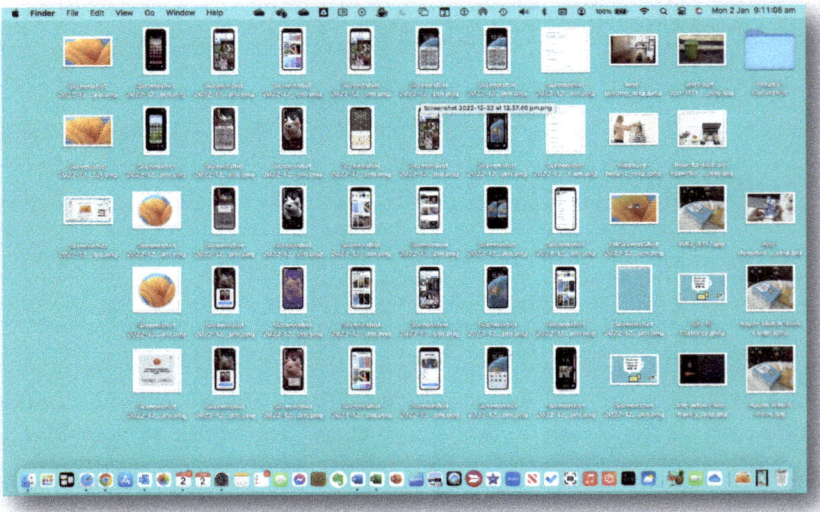

desktop, this can slow down your Mac significantly.

So, move them somewhere else! Either put them into a folder in *Finder* or take the opportunity to cull some no-longer needed files so that your Mac can focus!

Or use the **Stacks** feature described earlier in this document (in the section titled **Quickly Tidying a Messy Desktop**).

Fixing a Slow Mac

Do you have Adware/Malware

There are a couple of places I always check when dealing with a computer that is slow or behaving strangely.

They are the 'Library' areas of the Mac, under folders called 'LaunchDaemons' and 'LaunchAgents'.

First, in Finder, I check the **Macintosh HD -> Library** folders by these names

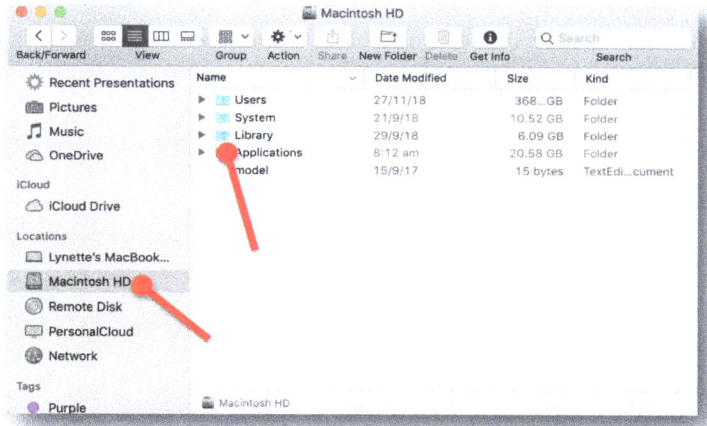

Then, also in Finder, I also choose **Go** (menu at top) **-> Go to Folder** ... and choose the **~/Library** folder, where I check the same folders.

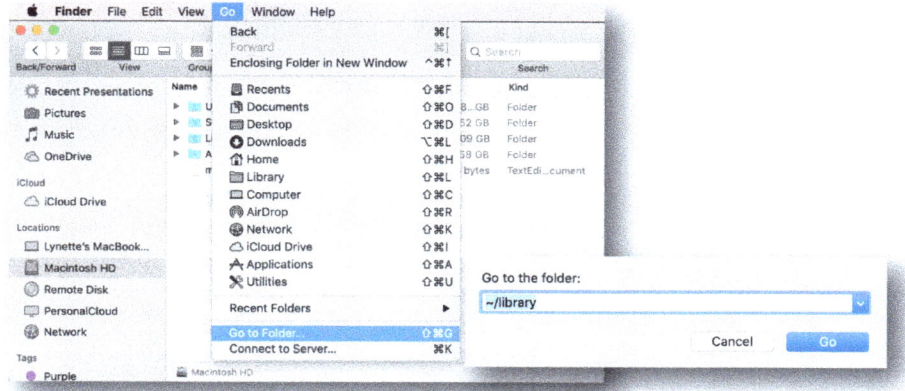

If I find anything there that I recognise as suspicious, I remove it from these areas.

Fixing a Slow Mac

I don't necessarily recommend that you do this yourself unless you truly understand what you are deleting.

A better way of seeking out and cleaning up such Malware and Adware is to use a product like **Malwarebytes** (described a bit earlier).

Check Activity Monitor for problem apps

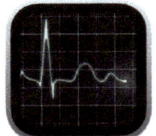

On my own Mac, I experienced some major issues that could not be resolved by any of the above 'fixes'.

My Mac would start up, then gradually 'freeze up' and get to the point where even the spinning beachball stopped spinning!

I discovered the source of my issue by checking a utility on my Mac - the **Activity Monitor**. The **Activity Monitor** showed that there was a particular process in the list of processes that was red and showed 'Not Responding'.

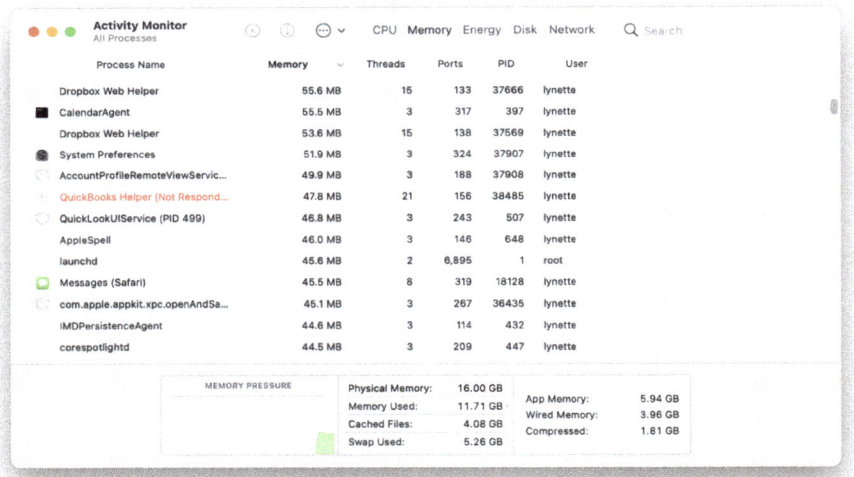

Those who are familiar with Windows, **Activity** Monitor is like the Windows 'Task Manager' on the Mac.

Activity Monitor can be opened from the **Launchpad** and can usually be found in in an App Group called **Other**.

Fixing a Slow Mac

Alternatively, **Activity Monitor** can be activated by using **Spotlight Search** at top right of your screen – click on the magnifying glass symbol, and then start typing **Activity Monitor**. Double-click on **Activity Monitor.app** item in the list (when it appears in the top section) to open this utility.

Activity Monitor shows what processes are using the Mac's CPU, Memory, Energy, Network (ie. data sent and received) and more.

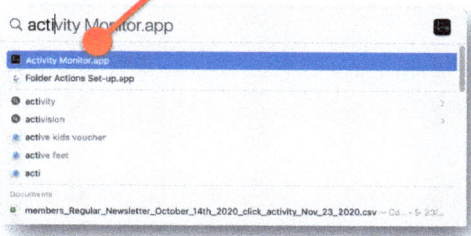

If the Mac is running slowly, click on **CPU** and/or **Memory** options along the top.

Click on the column heading for **%CPU** (in CPU tab) or **Memory** (in Memory tab) to sort by that heading, and thereby see the biggest 'hogs' that are currently running on your Mac.

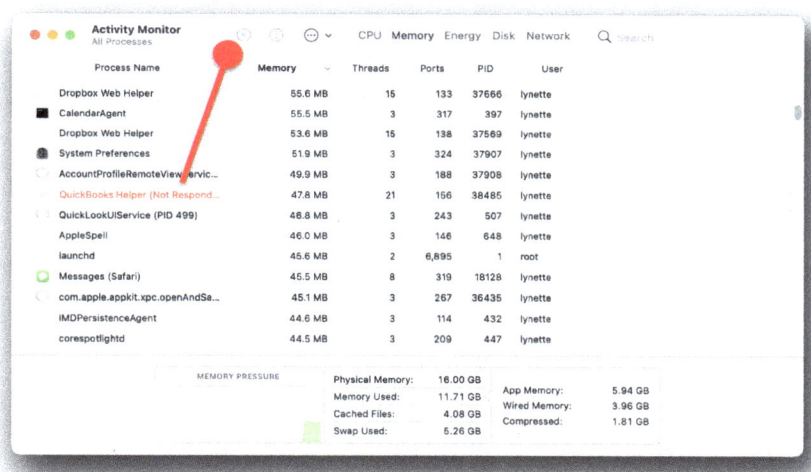

You may find a process in the list that shows that it is not responding or see one that doesn't need to be running so can be 'quit'.

Click on that process, then choose the ⊗ at the top (indicated) to **Quit** the process. If the process won't **Quit**, you may need to choose **Force Quit** instead.

In some cases, the app associated with the process may need to be uninstalled and re-installed to resolve the issue.

It is worth checking your own Activity Monitor for any such processes.

Other Books in this Series

A Guided Tour

Files, Folders & Finder

Backups, Apps and Settings

The Photos App

Videos about the Mac

Learn even more about your Mac with a range of Videos about the Mac, available on the iTandCoffee website.

For more information about iTandCoffee class videos and user guides, visit

www.itandcoffee.com.au/videos

www.itandcoffee.com.au/guides